C.E. THOM

HOW BiG WeRe THe
DiNOSAURS?

ILLUSTRATED BY
MARCY RAMSEY

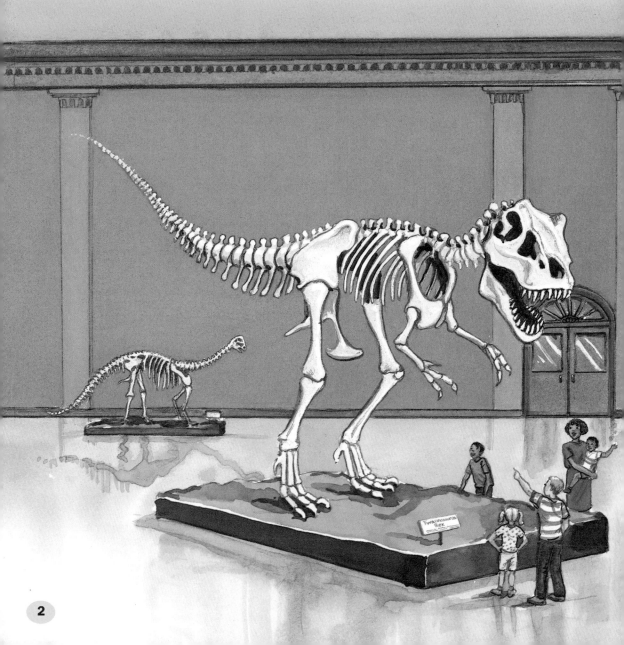

HOW BiG WeRe THe DiNOSAURS?

Some dinosaurs were huge animals. Tyrannosaurus rex (tye-RAN-uh-sawr-us rex) was much taller than a basketball hoop. Its head was larger than a shopping cart. You probably wouldn't be able to reach Tyrannosaurus's knees—even standing on your tiptoes.

Dinosaur scientists have found the bones of dinosaurs that were much smaller than Tyrannosaurus and also of dinosaurs that were even bigger. This book will help you find out how big dinosaurs were.

As you put together the dinosaur skeleton, you will learn about the bones and teeth of one of the great dinosaurs— the Tyrannosaurus rex. Follow the directions on pages 28 through 31.

WHAT WAS THE BIGGEST DINOSAUR?

Seismosaurus (SYZE-muh-sawr-us) is the biggest dinosaur that scientists know much about. This dinosaur was nearly half as long as a football field. It was taller than a five-story building. And it weighed almost 100 tons (90 metric tons)—about the same as forty cars.

Compsognathus
(komp-sog-NAY-thus) was
one of the smallest dinosaurs. It
was only as big as a chicken.

PALEONTOLOGISTS

Dinosaur scientists,
called paleontologists
(pay-lee-ahn-TAHL-uh-jists),
have found
giant bones—like
this one—from
Seismosaurus.

WHAT DiD DiNOSAURS EAT?

Most dinosaurs ate plants. The plant-eaters had flat teeth that helped them chew up leaves and branches.

Anatosaurus
(ah-NAT-uh-sawr-us)
ate fruits and seeds.

Apatosaurus
(ah-PAT-uh-sawr-us)
ate pine needles.

Triceratops
(try-SAIR-uh-tops)
ate bushes.

Dinosaurs that didn't eat plants are called meat-eaters.

Compsognathus ate insects and lizards.

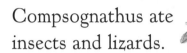

Oviraptor (oh-vi-RAP-tor) ate eggs, among other things.

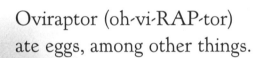

Tyrannosaurus rex ate other dinosaurs.

Meat-eating dinosaurs had long, sharp teeth and claws. Tyrannosaurus rex had the longest teeth—as long as your toothbrush!

DiD OTHER BiG ANiMALS LiVE AMONG THE DiNOSAURS?

No bears or elephants or whales lived when there were dinosaurs. But there were smaller animals: insects, fish, lizards, turtles, crocodiles, small animals that looked like mice, and birds.

Pteranodon (tair-AN-uh-don) looked like a dinosaur and a bird. It was a flying animal called a pterosaur (tair-uh-SAWR). Some pterosaurs were as small as sparrows. But Pteranodon was huge. Just one of its wings could stretch across your bedroom.

Dinosaurs lived millions and millions of years before there were any people. Their bones have been found in Africa, England, China, the United States, and many other countries.

WHY DID ALL THE DINOSAURS DIE?

No one knows for sure. But at the same time, other animals and many plants died, too.

Some scientists think that a meteorite, a gigantic rock from outer space, may have crashed into the earth. Dust from the crash could have blocked out the sun for years.

Without sunlight, plants couldn't grow. The dinosaurs would have starved— first the plant-eaters, then the meat-eaters.

HOW DO WE KNOW WHAT DINOSAURS LOOKED LIKE?

Paleontologists study fossils to find out about dinosaurs. Fossil bones are bones that have turned to stone in the ground.

People have found fossil teeth, eggs, and even footprints.

Footprints of a large meat-eater

HOW BiG ARe DiNOSAUR FOOTPRiNTS?

Seismosaurus left bathtub-size footprints. This huge dinosaur needed big legs and feet to carry its enormous body weight.

The small dinosaurs left small footprints. Some are shorter than your little finger.

Footprints of a small plant-eater

Footprints of a large meat-eater

Footprints tell paleontologists how fast the dinosaurs ran. The more space there is between each footprint, the faster the dinosaur was running.

Small, two-legged dinosaurs with slim legs—like Troödon (TROH-uh-don), shown here—were the fastest. They could run as fast as cars move on a city street.

WHY ARE DINOSAUR NAMES SO LONG?

Dinosaur names usually tell something about the dinosaur. The longer the name is, the more the name tells.

The longest dinosaur name is: MICRO · PACHY · CEPHALO · SAURUS (my-kro-pak-ee-SEF-uh-lo-sawr-us).

Micro, *pachy*, *cephalo*, and *saurus* are words from the Greek language. The words mean "small, thick-headed lizard."

About 150 years ago, the first dinosaur scientists thought that dinosaurs were a lot like lizards. That's when people began using the word *dinosaur*, which means "terrible lizard" in Greek. Paleontologists all over the world understand Greek words.

Micropachycephalosaurus

Minmi

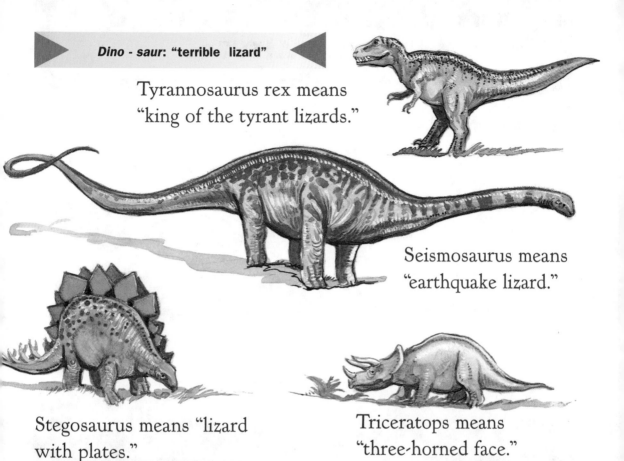

Tyrannosaurus rex means "king of the tyrant lizards."

Seismosaurus means "earthquake lizard."

Stegosaurus means "lizard with plates."

Triceratops means "three-horned face."

Sometimes a dinosaur is named after the person who discovered it or the place where it was discovered. The dinosaur with the shortest name is Minmi (MIN-my). It was named after the place in Australia where its fossil bones were found.

13

WHY DiD DiNOSAURS HAVE LONG TAiLS?

Long tails helped some of the dinosaurs walk on two legs. Tyrannosaurus rex's stiff, heavy tail balanced its huge head and helped it walk and run without falling over.

Seismosaurus's long tail balanced its long, thin neck. Its tail was as long as four minivans.

Some dinosaurs used their tails to protect themselves. Apatosaurus probably used its long, thin tail like a whip.

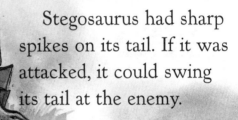

Stegosaurus had sharp spikes on its tail. If it was attacked, it could swing its tail at the enemy.

So could Ankylosaurus (ang·KYL·uh·sawr·us). The big, bony club at the end of its tail would have made quite a weapon. *Ouch!*

WHY DID SOME DINOSAURS HAVE SPIKES?

Some plant-eaters had this kind of armor for protection from the big, meat-eating dinosaurs. Knobby plates and bony spikes wouldn't have made a very tasty mouthful!

Nodosaurus
(no-do-SAWR-us)

Euoplocephalus
(yoo-op-lo-SEF-uh-lus)

Triceratops could use its horns like weapons. The horns over its eyes were longer than baseball bats.

Pachycephalosaurus (pak-ee-SEF-uh-lo-sawr-us) had a thick, bony cap on top of its head.

This hard-headed dinosaur used its head like a weapon. It fought other Pachycephalosaurs by ramming into them with its "crash helmet."

WHY DiD STEGOSAURUS HAVE PLATES ON ITS BACK?

No one knows for sure. The biggest plates were the size of garbage can lids. If they were covered with skin, a breeze blowing past them might have kept Stegosaurus cool.

The plates may have been covered with tough horn. The hard plates would have kept other dinosaurs from biting Stegosaurus.

WHAT SOUNDS DID DINOSAURS MAKE?

Dinosaur skeletons don't tell much about the parts of a dinosaur's throat that made sounds. So we don't know if dinosaurs roared or hissed or made chirping sounds like birds.

Parasaurolophus (par-ah-sawr-OL-uh-fus) had a long crest that was part of its nose. It's possible that this dinosaur could make a honking sound by blowing through the crest.

WHAT COLOR WERE DINOSAURS?

Fossil bones and teeth can't tell us what color dinosaur skin was. But fossil bones tell paleontologists that dinosaurs were like birds. Some birds are brightly colored, and others are a dull brown. Maybe that's the way dinosaurs were colored, too.

Ornitholestes (or-nith-uh-LES-teez) may have had spots or stripes to make it hard to see behind trees or through bushes.

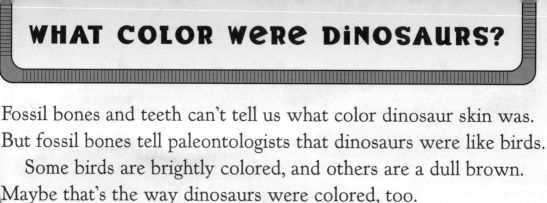

Stegosaurus

Ornitholestes

Dinosaurs with horns or spiky plates, like Triceratops and Stegosaurus, didn't need spots or stripes to help them hide.

Baby dinosaurs may have looked different from their parents. Grown-up Brachiosaurus was so big that it didn't have many enemies. But the babies may have had special marks or colors that helped them stay hidden from meat-eaters.

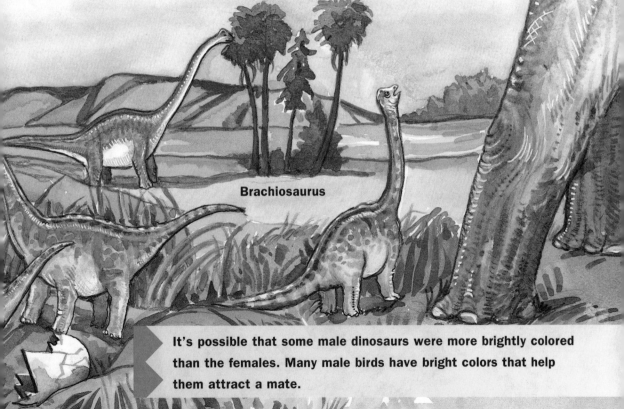

Brachiosaurus

It's possible that some male dinosaurs were more brightly colored than the females. Many male birds have bright colors that help them attract a mate.

HOW WERE BABY DINOSAURS BORN?

Baby dinosaurs hatched from eggs. Dinosaurs laid their eggs in nests on the ground.

Protoceratops (pro-to-SAIR-uh-tops) made a nest by digging a wide, shallow hole in the sand. It laid about eighteen eggs in the hole.

Then Protoceratops covered the eggs with sand and leaves to keep them warm—and to keep egg-eaters from spotting them.

Egg-eating
Oviraptor

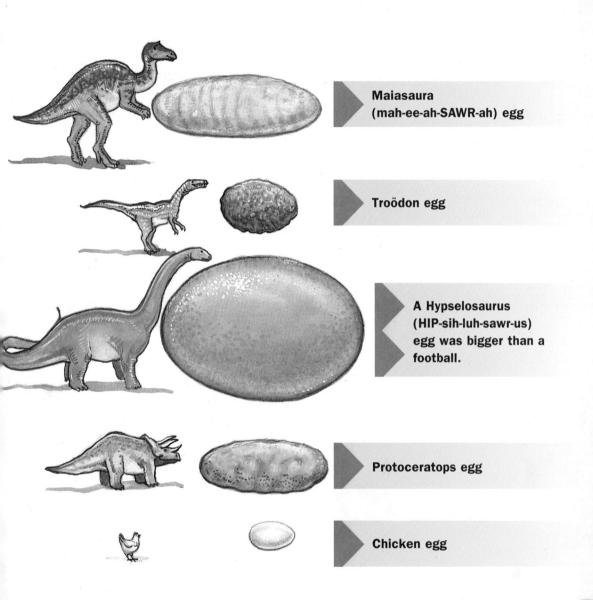

Maiasaura
(mah-ee-ah-SAWR-ah) egg

Troödon egg

A Hypselosaurus
(HIP-sih-luh-sawr-us)
egg was bigger than a
football.

Protoceratops egg

Chicken egg

HOW BiG WeRe BABY DiNOSAURS?

Some newly hatched dinosaur babies were smaller than squirrels. Some were much larger. A baby Apatosaurus was about the size of a fox terrier.

Mussaurus (moos-SAWR-us)   **squirrel**

Maiasaura   **cat**

Apatosaurus   **dog**

Dinosaurs took care of their babies. They brought food to them or herded the babies out of the nest to find food. When dinosaurs were on the move, they probably kept their babies safe in the middle of the herd.

Maiasaura

The name Maiasaura means "good mother lizard."

HOW MANY KiNDS OF DiNOSAURS WeRe THeRe?

Paleontologists have discovered about 350 different dinosaurs. But there were probably many more than that. There may have been more than 1,000 different kinds.

Not all the dinosaurs lived at the same time. Dinosaurs were the main animals on Earth for more than 100 million years. During that time some dinosaurs died out, and new kinds of dinosaurs came along.

Apatosaurus was as tall as the flagpole in front of your school.

Saltopus (SALT·o·pus) could fit inside your backpack.

Triceratops was about the size of a small school bus.

Dinosaurs came in many shapes and sizes. Now you know how big—and how small—the dinosaurs were!

Be a Junior Scientist!

You can be a junior scientist in your very own home. Turn your room into an excavation site. Assemble the dinosaur skeleton and examine the mighty Tyrannosaurus rex. Who knows? Maybe someday you will discover the reason for the extinction of dinosaurs!

INSTRUCTIONS

HEAD AND SPINE ASSEMBLY

1. Align the pegs on the right side of the skull with the holes on the left side of the skull and snap together.

skull bones

2. Align the front and tail section of the spine and snap together. Note: The tail will be sloping downward.

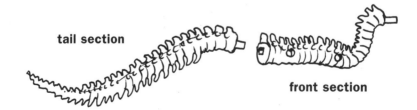

tail section

front section

LEG AND HIP BONE ASSEMBLY

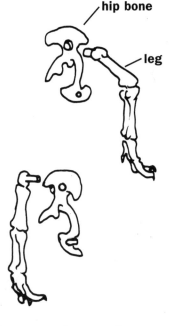

hip bone

leg

3. Slide the peg on the right leg through the hole in the right hip bone. Note: The right hip bone has two holes.

4. Slide the peg on the left leg through the hole in the left hip bone. Note: The hammer-shaped pieces of the right and left hip bones will be hanging down.

5. Holding the spine section with the tail facing you, insert the peg on the right side of the spine into the hole in the right leg. Repeat this step for the left side of the spine, inserting the left peg into the hole in the left leg. The two lower hammer-shaped pieces can now be snapped together.

The skeleton will now stand on its own.

FINAL ASSEMBLY

6. Hold the right half of the rib section so that the ribs are facing
    down and the arm is facing forward. Snap the two pegs into the
    corresponding holes on the right side of the spine. Repeat this
    step by snapping the two pegs on the left side of the rib cage
    into the corresponding holes on the left side of the spine.

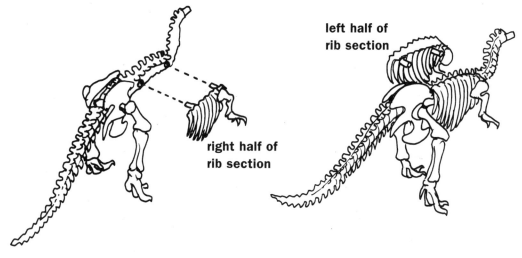

left half of
rib section

right half of
rib section

7. Find the hole at the base of the skull and snap onto the peg at the tip of the spine.

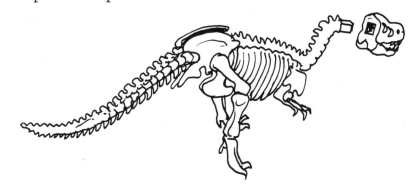

CAN YOU ANSWER THESE QUESTIONS?

Which footprint belongs to Apatosaurus? (pgs. 6, 11)

What did Triceratops have for protection? (pg. 16)

Which baby belongs to Maiasaura? (pg. 25)

Help Tyrannosaurus rex find its teeth. (pg. 7)